How to Study
the
BIBLE

PUBLISHING

Torrance, California

How to Study the Bible
© 2014 Bristol Works, Inc.

Rose Publishing, Inc.
4733 Torrance Blvd., #259
Torrance, California 90503 USA
www.rose-publishing.com

Printed in China by Regent Publishing Services Ltd.
May 2014, 1st printing

CONTENTS

WHY STUDY THE BIBLE?

The Bible is the most printed and read book in history. More evidence exists to confirm the Bible than to confirm any other ancient historical documents.

God's Word can change your heart and transform your life. The Bible wasn't written to be merely history or a piece of great literature. It is meant to be read with both the mind and heart. God loves you and wants you to love him.

"Man does not live on bread alone but on every word that comes from the mouth of the LORD."—Deuteronomy 8:3

Reasons to Study with Your Mind and Heart

To Know God

God created the heaven and the earth and everyone in it.

"In the beginning God created the heavens and the earth."—Genesis 1:1

"So God created mankind in his own image, in the image of God he created them; male and female he created them."—Genesis 1:27

To Enjoy and Love God

Meditate on God's character, principles, and promises. Rejoice in his love, care, and forgiveness. (Psalm 119:12–18, 160–162; 1 Timothy 6:17)

"Praise be to you, LORD; teach me your decrees. With my lips I recount all the laws that come from your mouth.

I rejoice in following your statutes as one rejoices in great riches. I meditate on your precepts and consider your ways. I delight in your decrees; I will not neglect your word."—Psalm 119:12–16

To Know God's Word

The Scriptures were inspired by God. They teach us the truth and show us what is wrong in our lives. They straighten us out.

"All Scripture is God-breathed and is useful for teaching, rebuking, correcting and training in righteousness, so that the servant of God may be thoroughly equipped for every good work." —2 Timothy 3:16–17

To Understand the Word

Jesus is called the Word because he is the ultimate communication from God. He existed from the beginning with God, he is God, and he created everything. He said that those who have seen him have seen the Father. (John 1:1–3; 10:30; 12:44–45; 14:7–9)

To Learn Direction in Life

The Bible shows us what to do.

"I have hidden your word in my heart that I might not sin against you." —Psalm 119:11

To Find Comfort and Hope

The Scriptures give us encouragement.

"For everything that was written in the past was written to teach us, so that through the endurance taught in the Scriptures and the encouragement they provide we might have hope."—Romans 15:4

To Let God Expose Our Innermost Thoughts and Desires

His Word helps us see ourselves as we really are and convicts us of sin so that we repent and change.

"For the word of God is alive and active. Sharper than any double-edged sword, it penetrates even to dividing soul and spirit, joints and marrow; it judges the thoughts and attitudes of the heart. Nothing in all creation is hidden from God's sight. Everything is uncovered and laid bare before the eyes of him to whom we must give account." —Hebrews 4:12–15

To Become Pure and Holy

Jesus prayed this for all believers that they would be set apart for God and his holy purposes.

"My prayer is not for them alone. I pray also for those who will believe in me through their message, that all of them may be one, Father, just as you are in me and I am in you. May they also be in us so that the world may believe that you have sent me."—John 17:20–21

To Obey the Great Commandment

The more we know God, the more we can love him. The Great Commandment is to love God with all of our being and our neighbor as ourselves (Mark 12:29–31). And Jesus gave us a new commandment to love one another.

"A new command I give you: Love one another. As I have loved you, so you must love one another. By this everyone will know that you are my disciples, if you love one another."—John 13:34–35

Examples in Scripture

- Moses read the Word of God to the people and commanded that it be read publicly. (Exodus 24:7; Deuteronomy 31:9–13)

- Joshua was commanded to meditate on God's word day and night. (Joshua 1:8)

- Kings of Israel were to study the Scriptures. (Deuteronomy 17:18–19)

- The longest psalm is a psalm about the value of knowing God's Word. (Psalm 119)

- Paul required his letters be read publicly. (Colossians 4:16; 1 Thessalonians 5:27)

- The apostle Paul urged Timothy to study the Word of God and handle it with care. (2 Timothy 2:15)

- The Ethiopian man was reading God's Word and he became a follower of Jesus. (Acts 8:27–40)

- Jesus read the Bible and taught it to the people. (Luke 4:16–21)

- Jesus said the value of studying the Bible was to see that it spoke about him. (John 5:39)

- God's Word is supposed to be close to the mouths and hearts of believers. (Deuteronomy 30:11–14; 32:47; Psalm 1:2; Romans 10:8–11; Colossians 3:16)

HOW TO BEGIN

Plan a Study Time

Decide on a quiet time and place to study God's Word and make it a daily habit, like eating. Some people get up early to spend time with God. Others study during the day or evening.

Pray

Ask God to help you understand his Word. Pray using your own words or something like this: "Lord, thank you for the Bible so that we will know who you are and what you want for our lives. Please help me understand it and do what you want me to do."

"Call to me and I will answer you and tell you great and unsearchable things you do not know."—Jeremiah 33:3

Read and Re-read It

The Bible is the most
important letter you
can ever receive—a
message from the
God of the universe
who made you, loves

you, and wants to communicate with
you. Open your "love letter" every day.
Re-read each chapter and verse several
times.

Know the Author

Read Genesis to learn about God who
created the world. All Scripture is
inspired by God. God actually visited
Earth in the form of man—the man
Christ Jesus. Jesus said, "I and my
Father are one" (John 10:30). Read the
Gospel of John to learn about God's
plan for you.

Take Notes

Write notes about what you read. Use a specific notebook or "spiritual journal" especially for Bible study. The three questions of "Inductive Bible Study" will help you look at the facts and discover how they apply to you. You might want to underline key verses or write notes in the margin of your Bible.

Make the Bible Your Authority

Accept and believe that what the Bible says is true. You may not understand everything in the Bible, but obey and apply what you do understand.

Find a Group

"As iron sharpens iron, so one person sharpens another" (Proverbs 27:17). God gave his Word to his people. When you share what you are learning with other fellow believers, God will do amazing things. It will also help you to be accountable to someone.

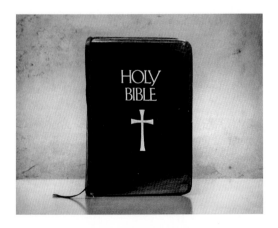

BASIC PRINCIPLES
OF BIBLE STUDY

Look for God's Overall Plan

God inspired approximately 40 people over a period of 1,600 years to write the 66 books of the Bible.

The Old Testament reveals God's loving plan of salvation, from Creation to prophecies of the future Messiah (the Savior).

The New Testament reveals God's salvation of sinful mankind by the suffering, death, and resurrection of the Messiah, Jesus Christ, and reveals the everlasting Kingdom of God.

Find the Background of the Books (five W's and one H)

Find out who wrote the books and the reason for, or theme of, the books. Ask "Who, What, Where, When, Why, and How?" Usually this information is in the first chapter or in the introduction to the book.

- Who wrote this book of the Bible?

- What is the book about? (Main themes)

- Where was it written?

- When was it written?

- Why was it written? (Occasion or purpose of the book)

GENESIS

Who: Moses

What: The Beginnings

Where: Egypt and Canaan

When: c. 1450 BC–1400 BC

Why: To demonstrate that God is sovereign and loves his creation.

Outline (Chapter)

- Creation, Fall, and Flood (1–11)
- Abraham (12–25)
- Isaac and Jacob (25–36)
- Joseph (37–50)

Key Verse: *I will establish my covenant as an everlasting covenant between me and you and your descendants after you for the generations to come, to be your God and the God of your descendants after you.* (Genesis 17:7)

JOHN

Who: John (The Beloved Disciple)

What: Gospel

Where: Asia Minor

When: c. AD 85–AD 95

Why: To show Jesus as the Son of God, the Word made flesh, who provides eternal life for all who believe in him.

Outline (Chapter)

- Introduction (1)
- Ministry of Christ (2–12)
- Private Ministry (13–17)
- Death and Resurrection (18–21)

Key Verse: *For God so loved the world that he gave his one and only Son, that whoever believes in him shall not perish but have eternal life.* (John 3:16)

Read Verses in Context

Read the surrounding chapters and the verses *before* and *after* the verse you are studying. Get the whole picture. Don't study verses out of context. Look at the outline of the book.

Whole Message of God's Word

Take the whole Bible as God's Word. Don't just concentrate on one verse or one idea. See if the teaching is explained more fully in other parts of the Bible.

Look at the small cross-references in your Bible to help you find other verses on the same subject. The following is an example of the cross-references and the verses around John 3:16.

12 If I have told you earthly things, and ye believe not, how shall ye believe, if I tell you of heavenly things?

13 And ^ano man hath ascended up to heaven, but ^bhe that came down from heaven, ^cthe Son of man which is in heaven.

14 And as Moses lifted up the serpent in the wilderness, even so must the Son of man ^abe lifted up.

15 That whosoever believeth ^ain him should not perish, but have eternal life.

16 For God so ^aloved the world, that he ^bgave his ^conly begotten Son, that whosoever ^dbelieveth in him should not perish, but have everlasting life.

17 For God ^asent not his Son into the world ^bto condemn the world; but that the world through him might be saved.

18 ^aHe that believeth on him is not condemned: but he that believeth not is condemned already, because he hath not believed in the name of the only begotten Son of God.

Cross references

13 a Pr 30:4; Deu 30:12; Ac 2:34
b Jn 3:31; 6:38
c Mt 8:20

14 a Jn 8:28; 12:34

15 a Jn 20:31; 1 Jn 5:11

16 a Ro 5:8; Eph 2:4; 1 Jn 4:10
b Ro 8:32; 1 Jn 4:9
c Jn 1:18; 3:18
d Jn 3:36; 6:40

17 a Jn 3:34; 5:36; 6:29; 20:21
b Jn 8:15; 12:47; 1 Jn 4:14

18 a Mk 6:16; Jn 5:24
b Jn 1:18; 1 Jn 4:9

Sample page of John 3:12–18
from a Bible with cross-references

Discover the Intended Meaning

As you read the Bible, look for the author's intended meaning.

- What did the author want to say?

- What did it mean in that culture?

- What does it mean now?

- What are the main ideas?

If you have questions, write them down, pray for insight, and discuss your ideas with others.

Learn the History and Geography

Use a time line to learn about the history of the Bible. Use maps to learn about the geography of where the events took place.

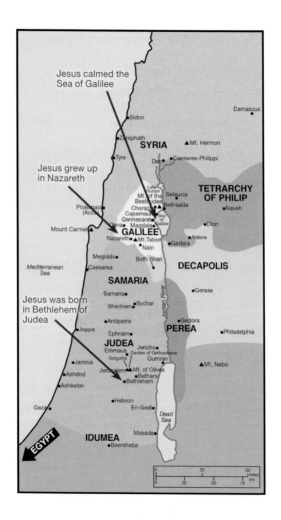

Jesus calmed the
Sea of Galilee

Jesus grew up
in Nazareth

Jesus was born
in Bethlehem of
Judea

Damascus

Sidon

Zarephath   SYRIA   ▲Mt. Hermon

Tyre   Dan   ●Caesarea-Philippi

Lake
Huldah   TETRARCHY
Mt. of the   OF PHILIP
Beatitudes   Seleucia
Chorazin Bethsaida   ●Naveh
Ptolemais Capernaum
(Acco)   Gennesaret Sea
Cana Magdala of Galilee
Mount Carmel▲   Dion
GALILEE   ●
Nazareth● ▲Mt.Tabor   Abilene
Nain   Gadara

Megiddo●   Beth Shan   DECAPOLIS

Mediterranean   Caesarea
Sea
SAMARIA   Gerasa
Samaria●   ●
Shechem● ●Sychar
Gedora
Antipatris●   PEREA
Joppa●   Ephraim●   Philadelphia●
JUDEA Jericho
Emmaus● ●Garden of Gethsemane
Golgotha   Qumran
Jamnia●   ▲Mt. Nebo
Jerusalem●▲Mt. of Olives
Ashdod●   ●Bethany
●Bethlehem
Ashkelon●
Hebron●
Gaza●   En-Gedi●   Dead
Sea
Masada●

EGYPT   IDUMEA
●Beersheba

Jordan River

0   25   50   miles
0   25   50   75   km

24

Figurative Language

Figures of speech are word pictures that help us understand a truth.

Metaphor

"Your word is a lamp for my feet, a light on my path" (Psalm 119:105) is a metaphor that helps us picture the Bible enlightening our minds and actions and giving us direction.

Simile

"As the deer pants for streams of water, so my soul pants for you, my God" (Psalm 42:1) is a simile that compares ideas with the words "like" or "as." Similes occur over 175 times in the Psalms.

Personification

Jesus used personification when he said if the people did not declare the mighty works they had seen God do, the stones would cry out in praise (Luke 19:40).

Hyperbole (Exaggeration)

Hyperbole is found in Matthew 5:29–30: "If your right eye causes you to stumble, gouge it out and throw it away. It is better for you to lose one part of your body than for your whole body to be thrown into hell. And if your right hand causes you to stumble, cut it off and throw it away. It is better for you to lose one part of your body than for your whole body to go into hell."

Forms of Literature

The Bible contains various forms of literature: History, Narrative, Poetry, Wisdom, Prophecy, Parables, and Letters. Recognizing each form will help you interpret the meaning. For example, parables explain a spiritual truth by means of a story or analogy. The parable of the Prodigal Son does not refer to a specific historical person but teaches that God is a loving father who joyfully welcomes back prodigal or rebellious children who later repent and return to him (Luke 15:11–32).

Summary of the Basic Principles

- Look for God's overall plan.

- Find the background of the book (who, what, where, when, why).

- Read verses in context.

- Take the whole message of God's Word.

- Discover the intended meaning.

- Learn the history and geography.

- Note figurative language.

- Notice the form of literature.

INDUCTIVE BIBLE STUDY

What does it say?

What does it mean?

How does it apply to me?

1. How can I find out for myself what the Bible says?

Read it and re-read the Bible passage. Read silently sometimes and read aloud other times. Don't start by reading what others have concluded about the Bible. Inductive reasoning moves from specific examples to general conclusions. Deductive reasoning moves from general examples to specific conclusions.

2. How can I know what the Bible means?

After reading the facts, you can summarize them. Don't jump to conclusions too fast. Read the passage several times and pray for wisdom. You will learn more and remember more if you discover what the Scriptures say yourself. Look at cross-references (other verses in Scripture that relate to the verses you read).

"If any of you lacks wisdom, you should ask God, who gives generously to all without finding fault, and it will be given to you."—James 1:5

3. How can I apply what the Bible says to myself?

The goal of Bible study is a transformed life and a deep relationship with God. Sometimes in Scripture, you will see a command to obey, an example to follow, a lesson to learn, or a sin to confess. Apply that to your life.

Other times, you will want to claim a promise, pray a prayer, forgive someone, or ask forgiveness. Listen to the "still small voice" of God. God says, "Be still and know that I am God."

As you listen and respond to God, you will be amazed at the results in your life as your relationship with him deepens.

"He makes wars cease to the ends of the earth. He breaks the bow and shatters the spear; he burns the shields with fire. He says, 'Be still, and know that I am God; I will be exalted among the nations, I will be exalted in the earth.'"—Psalm 46:9–10

WAYS TO STUDY

Jesus said: "I am the vine; you are the branches. If you remain in me and I in you, you will bear much fruit; apart from me you can do nothing" (John 15:5).

Reading the Bible is the best way to stay connected to God. Scripture reading is the lifeblood of the church. The Bible equips, trains, and empowers believers to fulfill God's calling.

Bible Studies

Study alone or with a partner. Small groups and home study groups can help you ask questions and share insights. Attend a Sunday School class or Bible Study at a Bible-teaching church.

Psalms and Proverbs

Read five Psalms and one chapter of Proverbs each day. (You'll read the 150 Psalms and 31 chapters of Proverbs in a month.)

Overview of the Bible

Read through the Bible in one year (about three chapters a day). One-Year Bibles and calendars give daily passages to read.

Listen to Learn

Listen to tapes of the Bible, radio programs that teach the Bible, and sermons that teach from the Bible. Taking notes is helpful.

Discuss the Bible with Others

Share what you've learned with others. Their questions will challenge you to pray and study more to find the answers.

Memorization

When scuba divers face problems under water, they rely on their previous training to find a way out. When we face temptation or sudden grief, our "training" will kick in.

All those verses we have memorized will come back; God will speak to us through them in unexpected ways.

One of the best ways to memorize something is by finding partners who help and challenge you to work together.

Reflection

It is often called meditation. It means that we allow the Bible to settle in our minds and hearts.

We do this by thinking about it all day long, wondering what a passage or a verse means for us throughout the day's activities.

Write a verse, or passage, on a small piece of paper and carry it along with you. If you are standing in line, waiting at a restaurant, or another short moment, take the paper out and think about how the text connects to your life at that specific moment.

Transformative Study

Studying the Bible does not mean one becomes an expert in one passage or book. Studying the Bible means we dig deeply so we can be deeply transformed.

The more we know about God, the more we can love him. God gave the Bible to the church. Reading and studying the Bible in community is most profitable.

You can read Scripture early in the morning, after meals, or before going to bed. Today there are many other opportunities for Bible reading, memorizing, and studying. The many hours we spend in transportation can be useful for listening to an audio recording of the Bible. The Internet is full of tools and help for Bible reading and studying.

Basic Passages to Study

Start with These Books

- ❏ Genesis
- ❏ John

Short Books

- ❏ 1 John
- ❏ 1 Thessalonians

Book Study: 11 More Books to Study

- ❏ Mark, Matthew, or Luke
- ❏ Acts
- ❏ Galatians
- ❏ Ephesians
- ❏ Philippians
- ❏ Colossians
- ❏ 2 Thessalonians
- ❏ 1 Timothy
- ❏ 2 Timothy
- ❏ Psalms
- ❏ Proverbs

Chapter Study: 11 Key Chapters

- ❏ John 1, 3, 4
- ❏ John 14, 15, 16, 17
- ❏ Romans 6, 8, 12
- ❏ Ephesians 5

Passage Study: 7 Key Passages

❏ The Fall of Man—Genesis 3
❏ The Ten Commandments—
   Exodus 20:1–17
❏ The Prophecy of the Coming Messiah—
   Isaiah 53
❏ The Beatitudes—Matthew 5:1–11
❏ The Sermon on the Mount—
   Matthew 5–7
❏ Two Great Commandments—
   Matthew 22:36–40
❏ The Prodigal Son—Luke 15:11–32

Verse Study: 17 Key Verses to Memorize

❏ Genesis 1:1
❏ Proverbs 3:5–6
❏ John 3:16
❏ John 1:9, 12
❏ Romans 3:23
❏ Romans 6:23

❏ Romans 5:8
❏ Romans 10:9
❏ Ephesians 2:8–9
❏ Acts 16:30–31
❏ Philippians 4:6–7
❏ Psalm 119:11

TOOLS FOR BIBLE STUDY

1. Study Bibles

A study Bible will help you a great deal. A study Bible will bring out the significance of God's Word. Study Bibles contain explanations, introductions, outlines, cross-references, and study notes. A good study Bible has a concordance, maps, and a topical index. Ask your pastor to recommend one.

Some examples of study Bibles:

- *ESV Study Bible*
  Crossway Books & Bibles

- *NIV Life Application Study Bible*
  Zondervan Publishers

- *NKJV Study Bible*
  Thomas Nelson Publishers

2. Concordances

A concordance helps you look up any word in the Bible. It gives an alphabetical listing of key words, names, and topics, plus a list of verses that contain that word. It locates all the occurrences of a word.

Some examples of concordances:

- *Strong's Exhaustive Concordance*
  Thomas Nelson Publishers

- *NAS Exhaustive Concordance*
  Broadman & Holman Publishers

- *NIV Exhaustive Concordance*
  Zondervan Publishers

3. Bible Software

Bible concordances and other references are available online. Enter a word or reference to quickly find and print out Bible verses in various versions.

Some examples of Bible software:

- Bible Gateway
  www.biblegateway.com

- Bible Hub
  www.biblehub.com

- The Unbound Bible
  www.theunboundbible.com

- The Blue Letter Bible
  www.blueletterbible.com

- Logos Bible Software
  www.logos.com

4. Bible Dictionaries

Look up words you don't understand, such as "grace," "redemption," or "faith." Expository dictionaries give you more detailed meanings and explanations.

Some examples of Bible dictionaries:

- *Holman Bible Dictionary*
  Broadman & Holman

- *New Illustrated Bible Dictionary*
  Nelson

- *Dictionary of the Bible*
  Eerdmans

- *New Unger's Dictionary*
  Moody Press

- *Zondervan's Pictorial Bible Dictionary*
  Zondervan

5. Bible Atlases, Maps, and Time Lines

On a map, locate *where* Bible events took place. Daniel was in Babylon. Babylon ruins are south of Baghdad today.

On a time line, locate *when* Bible events took place. During the fierce Assyrian Kingdom, around 781 BC, Jonah went to Nineveh to warn the people to repent.

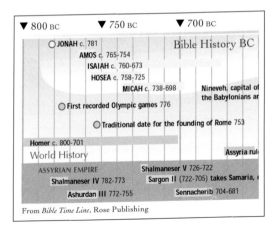

▼ 800 BC   ▼ 750 BC   ▼ 700 BC

○ JONAH c. 781   Bible History BC
   AMOS c. 765-754
   ISAIAH c. 760-673
   HOSEA c. 758-725
            MICAH c. 738-698   Nineveh, capital of
                                        the Babylonians ar
○ First recorded Olympic games 776

   ○ Traditional date for the founding of Rome 753

Homer c. 800-701
World History   Assyria rul

ASSYRIAN EMPIRE   Shalmaneser V 726-722
   Shalmaneser IV 782-773   Sargon II (722-705) takes Samaria,
   Ashurdan III 772-755   Sennacherib 704-681

From *Bible Time Line*, Rose Publishing

45

Some examples of Bible atlases, maps, and time lines:

- *Rose Then & Now Bible Map Atlas with Biblical Background and Culture*
  Rose Publishing

- *Atlas of Bible Lands*
  Broadman & Holman

- *NIV Atlas of the Bible*
  Zondervan

- *The New Moody Atlas of the Bible*
  Moody

- *Deluxe Then & Now Bible Maps* book
  Rose Publishing

- *Bible and Christian History Time Lines* book
  Rose Publishing

- *Bible Time Line* pamphlet
  Rose Publishing

6. Bible Commentaries and Handbooks

First, study the Bible yourself. See what it means and how it applies to you. List questions you have. Later, you can read to see how Bible scholars explain it.

Some examples of Bible commentaries:

- *Wycliffe Bible Commentary*
  Moody

- *Matthew Henry's Commentary*
  Zondervan

- *Eerdman's Commentary on the Bible*
  Eerdman

- *Zondervan Bible Commentary*
  Zondervan

- *Bible Knowledge Commentary*
  Nelson

- *Bible Exposition Commentary*
  Victor Books

Some examples of Bible handbooks:

- *Bible Overview*
  Rose Publishing

- *New Unger's Bible Handbook*
  Moody

- *Holman Bible Handbook*
  Broadman & Holman

- *Halley's Bible Handbook*
  Zondervan

7. Special Bibles

Topical Bibles organize Scripture into special areas of interest, such as Salvation, Marriage, or Prayer.

Interlinear Bibles compare original language (Hebrew or Greek) to modern language.

Large-print Bibles are easy to read and helpful for many people.

Some examples:

- *Nave's Topical Bible*
  Hendrickson Publishers

- *Topical Analysis of the Bible*
  Baker Book House Company

- *NIV Larger-Print Bible*
  Biblica

- *NIV Women's Devotional Bible*
  Zondervan

- *NLT Life Recovery Bible*
  Tyndale House

- *HCSB Apologetics Study Bible*
  Holman Bible Publishers

- *The Interlinear Hebrew-Greek-English Bible*
  Hendrickson Publishers

Building a Bible Reference Library

In addition, you will want to build a Reference Library. Check off each category as your library grows.

❏ Study Bible

❏ Concordance

❏ Bible Software

❏ Bible Dictionary

❏ Bible Atlas and Maps

❏ Bible Time Line

❏ Bible Commentary

❏ Bible Handbook

❏ Special Bible

S.O.I.L.
IN-DEPTH BIBLE
STUDY

Bible study is important to our growth as followers of Jesus. Jesus compares reading the Bible with a seed being planted in good soil. The seed planted in good soil represents those with an honest and good heart, who hear the word, apply it, and with patience, produce a crop or fruit.

"This is the meaning of the parable: The seed is the word of God. Those along the path are the ones who hear, and then the devil comes and takes away the word from their hearts, so that they may not believe and be saved. Those on the rocky ground are the ones who receive the word with joy when they hear

it, but they have no root. They believe for a while, but in the time of testing they fall away. The seed that fell among thorns stands for those who hear, but as they go on their way they are choked by life's worries, riches and pleasures, and they do not mature. But the seed on good soil stands for those with a noble and good heart, who hear the word, retain it, and by persevering produce a crop."
—Luke 8:11–15

SOIL

S = Selection

What do I study?

O = Observation

What do I see?

I = Interpretation

What does it mean?

L = Life Application

How does it apply?

Selection
What do I study?

---

1. Pray

   "Open my eyes that I may see
   wonderful things in your law."
   (Psalm 119:18)

2. Become Familiar with the Bible

   • The Old Testament was written
   before Jesus' birth and tells about
   the people of Israel and anticipates
   the coming of Jesus the Messiah.

   • The New Testament was written
   about Jesus' birth, life, ministry,
   death, and resurrection, and the
   years that followed as Christianity
   spread.

   • Know the type of book you are
   reading such as Law, Prophet,
   History, Poetry, and so on. This

can be found in the introduction to a Study Bible.

- Memorize the order of the Books of the Bible.

- Learn how to read the references:

For example: 2 Timothy 3:6

2 = Second letter or book

Timothy = Name of letter or book

3: = chapter

:6 = verse

3. Select the Passage

Determine where the passage begins and ends.

4. Select a Version

Decide on a translation such as the King James Version (KJV), the New International Version (NIV), the New Living Translation (NLT), the New King James Version (NKJV), or the New American Standard Bible (NASB).

There are many different Bible translations to choose from. Choose a version that is most helpful for the type of Bible study you will be doing.

The four main methods of Bible translation are:

- Word-for-Word
- Thought-for-Thought
- Balance
- Paraphrase

Word-for-Word

Scholars attempt to translate each word based upon the word usage at the time of the writing.

Examples:

- King James Version (KJV)
- New American Standard Bible (NASB)
- Revised Standard Version (RSV)

Thought-for-Thought (also known as "Dynamic Equivalence")

Scholars translate the meaning of each thought.

Examples:

- Good News Translation (GNT)
- New Living Translation (NLT)
- New Century Version (NCV)

Balance

A middle balance between a word-for-word and thought-for-thought approach.

Examples:

- New International Version (NIV)
- God's Word Translation (GW)

Paraphrase

A restatement of a translation in modern terms and vocabulary.

Example:

- The Message (MSG)

5. Remember the Four "Do-Nots"

- Do not "proof text" (take verses out of context).

- Do not be too literal (see Matthew 5:29–30).

- Do not ignore the Bible's cultural, historical, and literary background.

- Do not read your own ideas into the Scriptures.

Observation
What do I see?

1. Make Use of Tools

Study Bibles, commentaries, concordances, Bible dictionaries, Bible encyclopedias, interlinear Bible (Greek and Hebrew to English), Bible handbooks, and Bible atlases, time lines, and topical Bibles.

2. Observe the Text

- Do word studies. Observe words or expressions. Notice synonyms (words that have similar meanings) and antonyms (words that have opposite meanings). Pay attention to reoccurring words.

- Who are the people in the passage?

- What are the important ideas in the passage?

- Where are the places in the story?

- Pay attention to timespans.

- What is the literary genre (form), such as Narrative (story), Epic, Priestly Writings, Law, Liturgy, Poetry, Lament, Teaching, Prophecy, Gospel, Parable, Epistle (letter), or Apocalyptic literature?

3. Observe the Context

- What is the immediate context? What comes before and after the text?

- Who is talking? Who is listening?

4. Observe the Historical Setting

- When was this passage written?

- Where was this passage originally written?

- Who is the author? What is his occupation? What is his personality? Where is he from?

- Who is the original audience? To what nation do they belong? What is their history? Where do they live? Where are they from?

- What is the original purpose for this writing?

- Refer to maps, time lines, and other historical documents for more about the historical, sociological, and geographical setting.

Interpretation
What does it mean?

---

1. The Language Question

- What is the meaning of each word?

- What is the meaning in the original language (Hebrew or Greek)?

- How are significant words used elsewhere in Scripture?

- How does the genre affect the text?

- What is the form (such as the structure of the Abraham story in Genesis 11–25)?

- What is the sentence structure?

- Why are particular words used?

- Compare this passage to other versions of the Bible. (Use Bible websites that allow you to look up a passage in multiple translations side by side.)

2. The Historical Question

- How does the historical situation affect this text?

- How does the sociological situation affect this text?

- How does the geographical situation affect this text?

3. The Theological Question

- What truths are taught about the nature of God?

- What does this passage tell us about human nature?

- Does this passage have anything to say about sin?

- Does this passage teach truths about redemption and salvation?

- What does this passage have to say about the church and/or the Christian life?

4. The Tactical Question

- How does each paragraph fit into the author's reason for writing?

Life Application
How does this apply?

---

1. The Contemporary Question

- How do we apply what the author has said to the assumptions, values, and goals of our lives and society?

- What are the principles found in this passage that apply to the contemporary situation?

- How is God's redemption illustrated by this passage?

- Is there anything this passage has to say about certain social issues, such as racism, justice, poverty, or money?

2. The Personal Question

- How do we relate what the author says to our personalities?

- How do we relate this passage to our personal needs?

- How does this passage impact our families and close friends?

- What does this passage say about our moral decisions?

- How does the text affect our personal goals?

- How do these verses or principles apply to the church as a body?

Here are some things to keep in mind when reading the Old Testament:

1. **The Old Testament is as much the Word of God as the New Testament.**

   Though the Old Testament was compiled over hundreds of years and written by many different authors, it all originated with God. It is his Word to his people.

   The apostle Peter reminds believers, "We also have the prophetic message as something completely reliable.... No prophecy of Scripture came about by the prophet's own interpretation of things. For prophecy never had its origin in the human will, but prophets, though human, spoke from God as they were carried along by the Holy Spirit" (2 Peter 1:19–21).

2. The Old Testament helps us understand the New Testament.

The Old Testament deals with events and teachings hundreds—and even thousands—of years before Jesus was born. All of those events and teachings give us the background to all that happened when Jesus was born and during his life. For example, understanding the Old Testament sacrifices sheds light on what Jesus' sacrifice on the cross means. Knowing about the Old Testament prophecies of a coming Messiah helps us see how Jesus is that Messiah (the "Christ") who fulfills God's promises given long ago. The Old Testament laws, customs, and religious traditions help us make sense of Jesus' interactions with the Jewish religious leaders of his day.

3. God's grace for humanity is seen throughout the Old Testament.

As we read the Old Testament, we begin to understand the gracious and powerful God who created all things. We also understand the need for God's grace as we contemplate human folly and sin. Because of God's grace, rather than destroying humanity, God planned to save us.

We see this plan unfold in the pages of the Old Testament. It is not always a straightforward telling of God's plan. Often, we must carefully find God's plan in the stories of people who, just like us today, experience the goodness of creation, the corruption of a good creation, the terrible distorting power of sin, and the sad consequences of our separation from God.

4. Old Testament people and stories serve as examples for believers today.

The apostle Paul tells us that the things that happened to people in the Old Testament "happened to them as examples and were written down as warnings for us, on whom the culmination of the ages has come. So, if you think you are standing firm, be careful that you don't fall!" (1 Cor. 10:11–12).

Even the most faithful people in the Old Testament, like Moses and King David, fell into sin and were disciplined by God. Yet we see in the Old Testament how God continued to redeem and restore his people even after terrible sin and tragedy.

5. The Old Testament helps us recognize God's actions.

Although we are not of the world, Jesus has sent us to the world to be witnesses of his love, grace, and sacrifice. As long as we are in the world, we must learn to recognize the way God moves and acts in the world, through people, and sometimes in extraordinary ways that do not require people. The more we read the Old Testament, the more we learn to recognize God's ways in the world.

The Pentateuch (Law)

GENESIS
EXODUS
LEVITICUS
NUMBERS
DEUTERONOMY

The Pentateuch contains stories about the creation of the world, the flood, Abraham, Isaac, Jacob, the children of Israel in Egypt, the exodus, and the time the children of Israel spent in the wilderness before entering the Promised Land.

The books also record the law God gave to the people on Mt. Sinai which laid down the regulations for sacrifice, worship, and daily living. The Pentateuch is also called the Torah.

Historical Books

JOSHUA
JUDGES
RUTH
1 & 2 SAMUEL
1 & 2 KINGS
1 & 2 CHRONICLES
EZRA
NEHEMIAH
ESTHER

The Historical Books continue with the story of the people of Israel and the conquest of the Promised Land in the book of Joshua, the continuous cycle of disobedience in the book of Judges, the first kings and the United Kingdom, Divided Kingdom, the Assyrian invasion, Babylonian invasion, the years in exile, and the return from exile during the Persian rule.

Poetry & Wisdom

JOB
PSALMS
PROVERBS
ECCLESIASTES
SONG OF SONGS

The Poetry and Wisdom books include hymns, proverbs, poems, and dramas. They illustrate the creative ways the people of Israel expressed themselves to God and to each other.

These books deal with questions that affect humans everywhere and at any time: Questions about human suffering, death, what makes for a good life, knowledge for living. Poetry has a unique ability to express deep feelings and thoughts in effective and beautiful ways.

Prophetic Books

Major Prophets
Isaiah
Jeremiah
Lamentations
Ezekiel
Daniel

Minor Prophets
Hosea
Joel
Amos
Obadiah
Jonah
Micah
Nahum
Habakkuk
Zephaniah
Haggai
Zechariah
Malachi

The Major Prophets are not called "major" because of their message or quality, but rather because of the length of the books. The prophets brought God's words, which included warnings of judgment, warnings and hope for the immediate future (as well as warnings and hope for the distant future), and hope in the coming Messiah.

The Minor Prophets, also called "The Book of the Twelve" in the Hebrew Bible, are just as important as the Major Prophets. They are called "minor" because of the shorter length of the books. They also brought God's word to the people regarding judgment and hope.

Between the Old Testament and the New Testament

An approximate 400-year gap divides the events in the Old Testament and the birth of Jesus in the New Testament.

The Old Testament ends around 400 BC when many Jews returned to Jerusalem from their exile in Babylon. They returned to rebuild the city and the temple.

This 400-year gap is known as the Intertestamental Period (meaning "between the testaments") or the Second Temple Period (referring to the time after the temple was rebuilt).

READING THE NEW TESTAMENT

The events in the New Testament take place in a time of political difficulties. The Roman Empire had tightened its fist around regions like Judea, with people unwilling to bow down to the Roman emperors. Many Jews hoped and prayed for a liberating Messiah to come and drive the Romans away from Jerusalem and rebuild the kingdom of David.

God did send the Messiah, but he was not the Messiah they were expecting. He is much more than a political leader: he is the Savior who conquered death, defeated evil and sin, allows us a direct relationship with God, and offers eternal life.

The New Testament tells us the story of this Messiah, Jesus Christ, his life, teachings, death, and resurrection.

The New Testament consists of twenty-seven books.

- The four Gospels narrate the life of Jesus Christ—his birth, ministry, death, and resurrection.

- The book of Acts tells the story of the first Christians.

- The twenty-one epistles are letters from early church leaders to churches and believers. Letters from the apostle Paul make up most of the epistles in the New Testament.

- The book of Revelation is unique in the New Testament because it is the only book that is written in an apocalyptic style; it relates its message through signs, symbols, dreams, and visions.

The Gospels

MATTHEW
MARK
LUKE
JOHN

The term *gospel* was used in the Roman world as an imperial proclamation, the good news of the deeds of the Caesar. However, in the New Testament, the good news these books present is about "Jesus the Messiah, the Son of God" (Mark 1:1).

The Gospels tell a story about the actions and teachings of Jesus. In his life and words, Jesus proclaimed the coming of God's kingdom. God's promises to his people in the Old Testament are now fulfilled in Jesus.

However, we do not find just one story about Jesus. Rather we find four similar yet distinctive stories. Matthew, Mark,

Luke, and John tell us about Jesus' life and work from four related perspectives. Why are there four Gospels instead of just one? One answer is that it takes four points of view to get the whole story about Jesus. Some might argue that one authoritative story should be enough. However, God chose to reveal himself using four Gospels.

The Gospel of John begins with these words: "In the beginning was the Word … and the Word became flesh" (1:1, 14). God chooses as his preferred method of communication to speak to humans by means of the human. This is true of the Bible and it is supremely true of Christ whom we are told is God in the flesh (John 1:14–18). So then, the Gospels are, like Jesus, both a Divine work as well as a human work. They have real human authors and one divine Author. They give details that might be difficult to understand, but they are never truly contradictory. They have four different points of view on the history of Jesus, but only one Divine conclusion as to his identity as the Son of God.

Gospel	Audience	Jesus the Son of God
MATTHEW	Jewish world	Is the Messiah King of Israel
MARK	Greek-speaking world	Is the Power of God in the world
LUKE	Gentile world	Is the Ideal Man of God
JOHN	Whole world	Is the Word of God

The Book of Acts

The book of Acts is a natural continuation of the Gospels. The good news of Jesus continues in the work of Jesus' disciples in Jerusalem and throughout the world. In the book of Acts we find God's plan for humanity being played out in the life of the early Christians, who embodied Jesus' ministry and announced the good news of salvation to all peoples.

Similar to the Historical Books in the Old Testament, the book of Acts gives identity to God's people today by showing us how God's mission spread to all people and nations of the world.

Although the apostles Peter and Paul play a significant role in the book, the main characters of the book are God and the church. The apostles Paul and Peter lay the foundations for the spread of the gospel and illustrate the ministry of the Holy Spirit through the apostles.

Acts tells about the spread of the gospel. For that reason, some knowledge of the places Christians visited and of the cultures in those places helps us to better understand the importance of the book.

The Four Purposes of the Book of Acts

1. **Proclamation:** The book of Acts proclaims the good news of Jesus Christ. It presents the gospel message.

2. **Apologetic:** It defends Christianity as a source of blessing.

3. **Unifying:** It shows the importance of preaching the gospel to both Jew and Gentile alike.

4. **Teaching:** It's a book of instruction for believers. The history of the book of Acts is the history of God's people.

The Letters

Letters written by the apostle Paul

ROMANS

1 & 2 CORINTHIANS

GALATIANS

EPHESIANS

PHILIPPIANS

COLOSSIANS

1 & 2 THESSALONIANS

1 & 2 TIMOTHY

TITUS

PHILEMON

Other letters

HEBREWS

JAMES

1 & 2 PETER

1, 2 & 3 JOHN

JUDE

The letters (or epistles) make up twenty-one of the twenty-seven books in the New Testament. They contain vital information for Christians and their journey through life. Whereas the Gospels present the good news of Jesus—his life and ministry—the epistles explain the effects of Jesus' ministry, the coming of the Holy Spirit, and the spread of the gospel through Jerusalem, Judea, Samaria, and the Gentile world.

There are different kinds of epistles in New Testament:

1. Personal letters, such as Philemon which is written to a specific individual.

2. Circular letters, such as Ephesians which was a letter meant to be circulated among several churches in a region.

3. Letters to a specific congregation, such as 1 and 2 Corinthians which were written to the church congregation in the city of Corinth.

4. Other letters do not name the author or the recipients, such as Hebrews which does not name its author and 1 John which does not indicate to whom it is written. Others look only in a very general way like a letter at all (James).

However, all the letters share some important features. The first, and most important, is that they are divine communications for God's people in the early church and throughout history.

Another important consideration about these New Testament letters is that they are occasional documents. This means that each letter was written to address a specific set of issues, at a specific time, and in a specific place. This point is important to keep in mind because it highlights the value in knowing as much about the context of the letter as possible. It also reminds us that none of the letters, or even all of them put together, represents the full theology of Paul, Peter, or John. Rather, they were addressing specific issues. Those issues determined the content of each letter.

However, understanding the issues that each letter addresses is not easy. Often, reading the letters can feel like listening in on a person's phone conversation; we know only half of it.

The Book of Revelation

The book of Revelation is not an epistle. Rather it belongs to a special category or genre of writing, known as apocalyptic literature. Apocalyptic is a type of literature that reveals God's plans that had been hidden to humanity. The message is conveyed through signs, symbols, dreams, and visions.

Interpreting the book has always been a great challenge for Christians. However, its message is much too important to simply ignore it. We must approach the book with a sense of respect and wonder, but also with the confidence that God's message in the book is still relevant to all believers today.

Despite the many disagreements about the meaning of the book, there are important agreements among Christians:

- The message of the book is relevant for Christians today, as it was for Christians in the times of the apostles.

- The main purpose of the book is to provide hope and encouragement for believers at all times, especially in times of persecution or suffering.

- The message of the book is clear on at least three points: (1) Christ is coming back and will judge humanity; (2) the powers of evil are doomed before Christ; and (3) God promises a wonderful future for all who believe in Christ.

MORE RESOURCES

Good Books on Bible Study

Discipleship Journal's Best Bible Study Methods by Munro & Couchman (NavPress, 2002)

How to Study Your Bible by Kay Arthur (Harvest House, 2001)

How to Study The Bible by R. A. Torrey (Whitaker House, 1986)

How to Study The Bible and Enjoy It by Skip Heitzig (Tyndale House, 2002)

Rick Warren's Bible Study Methods by Rick Warren (Zondervan, 2006)

How to Get the Most from God's Word by John MacArthur, Jr. (Word Publishing, 1997)

How to Read the Bible For All Its Worth by Gordon D. Fee and Douglas Stuart (Zondervan, 1982)

Bible Study Made Easy by Mark Water (Hendrickson Publishers, 1992)